Quick
&
easy

Gerbil

Care

Sue Fox

Photo Credits

Isabelle Francais: 45
Michael Gilroy: 1, 4, 5, 6, 9, 11, 13, 15, 18, 21, 22, 30, 35, 36, 46,
    51, 55, 54, 57, 61
Horst Mayer: 12, 29
John Tyson: 47

T.F.H. Publications, Inc.
One TFH Plaza
Third and Union Avenues
Neptune City, NJ 07753

Printed and Bound in China
    07 08 09   3 5 7 9 8 6 4

ISBN13 978-0-7938-1028-4

Library of Congress Cataloging-in-Publication Data
Fox, Sue, 1962-
    Quick & easy gerbil care / Sue Fox.
    p. cm.
    Includes index.
    ISBN 0-7938-1028-0 (alk. paper)
1.Gerbils as pets. I. Title: Quick and easy gerbil care. II. Title.
    SF459.G4F69 2004
    636.935'83--dc22

                                    2004013924

This book has been published with the intent to provide accurate and authoritative
information in regard to the subject matter within. While every reasonable precaution
has been taken in preparation of this book, the author and publisher expressly disclaim
responsibility for any errors, omissions, or adverse effects arising from the use or
application of the information contained herein. The techniques and suggestions are
used at the reader's discretion and are not to be considered a substitute for veterinary
care. If you suspect a medical problem, consult your veterinarian.

The Leader In Responsible Animal Care For Over 50 Years!™
www.tfh.com

Table
of Contents

1	You and Your Gerbil	5
2	Housing Your Gerbil	21
3	Feeding Your Gerbil	35
4	Taming and Activities for Your Gerbil	45
5	Gerbil Health Care	51
	Resources	63
	Index	64

You and Your Gerbil

Congratulations on your decision to bring a gerbil into your home as a pet! Gerbils are brave, curious, and friendly companions who will bring much joy to your family.

Natural History

The Mongolian gerbil (*Meriones unguiculatus*) is the gerbil species most often kept as a pet. The Mongolian gerbil is also known by the names of Mongolian desert gerbil, clawed gerbil, and clawed jird, but its scientific name, *Meriones unguiculatus*, is always the same.

The gerbil is native to the desert and semi-desert areas of Mongolia and northeastern China.

The Mongolian gerbil is native to the desert and semi-desert areas of Mongolia and northeastern China. Mongolian gerbils are social animals and live in family groups of related individuals. However, they are territorial and will attack an unrelated or unfamiliar gerbil that tries to enter their territory.

The home range for the Mongolian gerbil can encompass almost one-half of a mile. The need for a large home range is probably due to the desert environment in which the gerbils live; gerbils probably need to forage long distances in order to find sufficient food.

Their burrows extend underground to a depth of about two feet. This depth helps to moderate the temperatures so that their burrows stay relatively cool when it is hot above ground and warm when it is cold above ground. The gerbils maintain a tidy orderliness in their burrows. They have separate nesting chambers, food storage rooms, and bathroom areas.

Wild gerbils are colored so that they blend into their desert habitat. The dense fur on their back is a golden sandy color and the fur on their belly is pale gray. Like a kangaroo, gerbils have long muscular hind legs that enable them to hop and leap quickly. Their front legs are shorter and are used to hold food and to dig.

Wild gerbils are preyed on by a variety of animals, including birds of prey and snakes. Therefore, gerbils warn each other of

Quick & Easy Gerbil Care

approaching danger by drumming their hind feet on the ground. Even though their ears are small, gerbils have acute hearing. Their large eyes help them to see when foraging at night.

Introduction to Pet Life

During the early 1900s, many scientists and medical researchers were interested in obtaining new species of rodents for use as laboratory animals. From the start, the Mongolian gerbil received special notice by scientists because it was naturally gentle and not as likely to bite. However, even though the Mongolian gerbil and the Syrian hamster began life in captivity as laboratory animals, they are now kept as pets all over the world.

In 1935, a Japanese scientist caught 20 pairs of Mongolian gerbils from the Amur River basin located on the border of China and Russia. The gerbils readily bred in captivity and proved useful laboratory animals. In 1954, four breeding pairs were sent from Japan to the US and 24 breeding pairs were sent to Great Britain in 1964 by the US. In such a fashion, laboratory colonies of Mongolian gerbils were established in various countries around the world.

Natural Habitat

The 81 known species of gerbils are found in desert areas throughout Africa, parts of Europe, and across Asia into China. Most gerbils live in arid climates in desert habitats. The Mongolian gerbil, the species kept most often as a pet, comes from the deserts and plains of Mongolia and other provinces of China.

Very hot summers and very cold winters are typical of this gerbil's natural habitat. Gerbils adapt well in order to be able to survive the severe desert environment, living in an underground network of burrows, foraging for food both at night and during the day, storing food, and deriving water metabolically from the foods they eat.

A Useful Tail

Gerbils measure about nine inches in length, including their long, fur-covered tail, which helps them keep their balance when they sit up. This tail also helps them to leap and turn when pursued by a predator. If a gerbil is grabbed by the black tuft at the tip of his tail, he will lose the skin, exposing the vertebrae, and the tuft will not re-grow.

Gerbils were first available as pets in North America in 1964, and they have been increasingly popular as pets since then. Their inquisitive nature, calm demeanor, and clean habits have made them appealing to potential pet owners.

Characteristics of the Pet Gerbil

Gerbils are ideal small pets. Gerbils are cute, easy to care for, and practically odorless. Even though they are lively and agile, gerbils are docile, gentle pets. Unlike other small pets, such as hamsters, they are not timid and nervous. Brave and curious, gerbils will eagerly explore your hand or anything else put near them. Instead of running away from something unknown, an alert and inquisitive gerbil will often advance and investigate. In new situations, a gerbil will stand on his hind legs, using his tail for assistance, and will sniff the air to investigate.

Gerbils are often content to be left alone in their cage for long periods of time, such as when you are at work or school. They can even remain unattended in their cage with extra food and water over the weekend. Their relatively small size makes them easy for children to hold and play with, and they are not intimidating. Gerbils can be very affectionate and learn that their owner represents food and playtime. They will stand up on their hind feet to greet their owner. However, gerbils are not cuddly pets. Although

Quick & Easy Gerbil Care

they like to be petted, they also like to bounce around and play rather than being held for long periods of time.

Gerbils are also territorial, and adult gerbils placed together in a cage for the first time will often fight. Both males and females produce a yellow-brown musty-smelling secretion from a gland on their belly that marks their territory. The gland is not conspicuous; it looks like a small hairless patch. The gland scent is most obvious to other gerbils, so you are unlikely to notice the smell. By sniffing each other's belly, gerbils can tell familiar from unfamiliar gerbils and whether a gerbil is male or female. Gerbils mark items in their cage with their scent by rubbing their belly on them. They also mark other gerbils with their scent. When a gerbil mounts another gerbil of the same sex, he or she is actually marking the other gerbil, not mating. Gerbils also mark their territory with urine and droppings.

One of their favorite pastimes is digging and burrowing through the bedding in their cage. They are not trying to escape though; they are indulging in their instinctive urge to dig. Unless your gerbil cuts himself on the wire in a cage corner, this activity is nothing to be concerned about. Providing your gerbils with more toys will sometimes reduce this repetitive behavior.

It is part of a gerbil's natural instincts to dig and burrow in his bedding or cage materials.

You and Your Gerbil

Choosing a Gerbil

A pet store is a good place to buy gerbils. Make sure the store is clean, the staff is knowledgeable, and the animals are healthy. You can also obtain a gerbil from a humane society or from gerbil breeders. Before you buy your gerbils, you should purchase their cage and supplies and have everything ready prior to bringing home your new pets.

Finding a Healthy Gerbil

A healthy gerbil should have dense, shiny fur. The coat should be smooth and sleek, with no bald areas or flaky skin. The gerbil's eyes should be clear and bright, and he should look a little plump.

When you hold the gerbil, he should feel solid, not frail. Do not choose an animal that is listless, has runny eyes, a runny nose, a rough or thin coat, lumps, or scabs. Dirty, matted fur near a gerbil's tail could be a sign of diarrhea. Look at the inside of the gerbil's front feet. Because sick gerbils wipe their nose on the inside of their front feet, check to be sure the fur in these areas is not wet or matted, which would indicate a sick gerbil.

A healthy gerbil is active and curious. He should not limp or move awkwardly. A good choice is a gerbil that is bold and inquisitive and

Gerbil Talk

Gerbils have many interesting behaviors. They communicate with each other by squeaking and by thumping their back legs during courtship, playing, and when alarmed. Gerbils are even-tempered and not easily provoked to bite. However, if they feel threatened or frightened, they might stamp their hind leg as a sign that they will bite if you do not stop your threatening behavior.

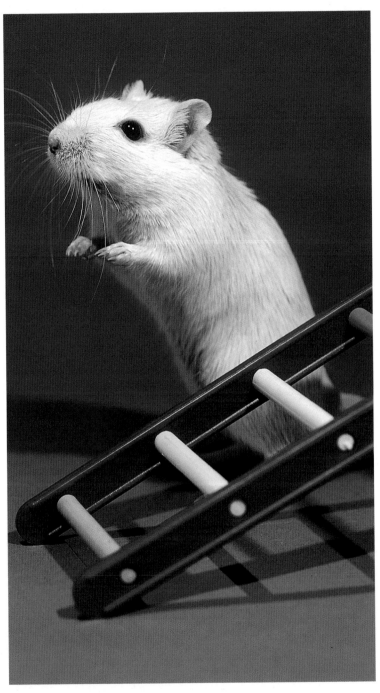

A healthy gerbil is friendly, active, and curious.

You and Your Gerbil

If you are obtaining young gerbils, make sure they are at least four weeks of age. These 17-day-old babies are not ready to leave their mother yet.

investigates your hand when you place it in the cage. A gerbil that climbs onto your hand will make a good pet. Do not choose a gerbil that runs and hides, struggles frantically, or is aggressive and tries to bite.

Choose your gerbils from a clean, spacious cage. Gerbils that come from a dirty, crowded environment are less likely to be healthy.

Age

It's best to pick young gerbils, because they will be easier to tame and will most likely live longer than an older animal. Gerbils are weaned from their mother at about three weeks of age and are ready to go to their new homes at four weeks of age. Therefore, it is best to buy a gerbil that is between four and eight weeks of age or about two to three inches in body length.

How Many?

The best situation is to buy a pair of gerbils. A gerbil kept alone may be less happy and may not thrive. A mixed pair (that will, naturally, produce young) or two females get along best, but it's best not to get a mixed pair unless you plan to house the babies yourself or find homes for them. Males tend to fight as they get older, but they may get along okay if you obtain them both together at a young age.

If you get a pair, obtain the gerbils at the same time so they can grow up together. Adult gerbils (about twelve weeks old) are territorial and will fight if another gerbil is introduced into their home. A pair of gerbils will form a lifelong bond. They will wrestle and play fight together, taking turns chasing each other around their cage. The two gerbils will also groom one another and curl up to sleep together.

Keeping more than two gerbils together in the same cage is not recommended. A third gerbil is likely to bullied by the other two gerbils.

Male or Female?

Male gerbils are larger than females and have a somewhat stronger odor due to their scent secretions. However, if their cage is regularly cleaned, the odor is not readily detected by people.

Young male gerbils can be differentiated from females by their dark-colored scrotum, located near the base of their tail. This difference is easier to detect in adult gerbils. If you are buying young gerbils,

It's best to buy a pair of gerbils who are approximately the same age.

Gerbil Relatives

Sometimes other species of gerbils are offered for sale by pet stores. These include the fat-tailed duprasi, pallid gerbil, Persian jird, and Shaw's jird. Some of these species are smaller than the Mongolian gerbil, while a few are larger.

Do not house different species of gerbils together, as they are likely to fight. The housing requirement for most species of gerbils is the same: Larger species should be provided with a correspondingly larger cage. However, the dietary requirements can vary. In some cases, live foods such as mealworms must be regularly offered.

Additional information on species requirements can be found on websites devoted to gerbils and their care. If you know the species' scientific name, the library is also a good source of information on diet. Ideally, the pet store employees should be able to alert you to any differences in care from that needed by the Mongolian gerbil.

the only way you may be able to determine the sex of a gerbil is by comparing it to the cage mates. The distance between the anus and the genital papilla will be much greater in the male than in the female. You might also notice a slight swelling where the male's scrotum will be. The female also has nipples, but these can be difficult to see. Blowing on the gerbil's belly can part the hair enough to detect the nipples. The breeder or employees of the pet store or humane society should be able to help you determine the sex of your gerbil.

Be aware that a female might be pregnant if she was not separated soon enough from the males. Gerbils can first breed between 10 to 12 weeks of age. Baby gerbils are born pink and hairless with their eyes closed after a gestation period of 25 to 28 days. Usually, 4 to 6 gerbils are born in a litter, but as many as 12 gerbils in one litter have been reported. Because of this possibility, try to buy your gerbils from a source where the females are kept separate from the males. If this is not possible, check to see whether the pet store employees know how old the gerbils are, and then you can determine the likelihood of a female being pregnant.

If you decide to keep a male and female gerbil together, you can expect your pets to constantly have babies. However, this is not a decision to be taken lightly. You must consider whether you are able to find new homes for all of the babies. Pet stores might be interested, but they might not always need gerbils when you are trying to find new homes for your weaned gerbils. If you are going to breed gerbils, consider choosing gerbils with the less common colors, as pet stores are often more interested in such varieties.

Color Varieties

All small animals kept in captivity, including rats, mice, hamsters, rabbits, and guinea pigs, eventually develop mutations from their normal color. Such mutations are rare. It is thought that in the wild, animals that are unusual in color are more noticeable by predators and do not live long enough to reproduce. In pets, a more conspicuous color is not a problem, because people protect pets from potential predators.

Gerbils are available in more than a dozen color varieties, including black, such as displayed on this male.

Hobbyists have increased the prevalence of color mutations by selectively breeding gerbils with desirable colors. By learning about genetics and carefully keeping track of the results of certain pairings, breeders are able to develop new color mutations.

Besides the standard wild agouti color, gerbils are available in more than a dozen attractive colors, including black, golden, cream, gray, and Burmese, which looks similar in color to the Burmese cat. Gerbils also come in what are known as "marked colors," which means they have patches of color on a solid background. Mutations in coat length and texture have not yet appeared, although they are likely to develop in the future.

Bringing Home Your New Pet

After selecting your gerbils, be sure to ask the breeder or store employee to show you how to properly hold them. It is important that you are comfortable handling your pets before you leave the pet store or breeder.

Ask the pet store employee or breeder to place a small handful of shavings from the gerbils' cage into the box you are using to take them home. Place the old shavings into your pets' new home. The smell of their original home can help your gerbils settle more comfortably into their new environment. If your new pets' home is not yet set up for their occupancy, have someone else watch them

Long Live the Gerbil

Gerbils live to be about three to five years old. Make sure that once the novelty of owning gerbils wears off, you will still be interested in caring for your pets. Unenthusiastically caring for your gerbils, or worse, neglecting them, is not fair. Be sure that you will still be interested in caring for gerbils years from now.

Quick & Easy Gerbil Care

Single Gerbils

If you cannot obtain more than one gerbil, be sure to give your single gerbil plenty of attention and exercise.

while you arrange their new quarters. Gerbils can quickly chew out of the cardboard box provided by pet stores for the trip to your home.

Introducing Gerbils to Each Other

If your gerbil is an addition to the one (or pair, or group) that you already have, it's necessary to make the proper introductions. You should probably not just place a new gerbil into your pet's cage and expect all to be well. Gerbils are territorial and often do not accept an unfamiliar gerbil.

A new cage is often an unanticipated cost to purchasing a new gerbil. It is important that the cage or cages you use for the introduction be new. Your original gerbil will resent any newcomer's intrusion into his territory. He will be very aggressive in defense of his home, and the success of pairing him with a new gerbil will be reduced.

Choose a younger gerbil to increase the chances for success. Younger gerbils tend to be more readily accepted than another adult.

Several methods can be used to facilitate the introduction. Place your original gerbil in a wire cage, and place the new gerbil in another wire cage. Slide the two cages together, so the gerbils can smell each other through the cage bars.

Alternatively, you can try dividing a wire cage or aquarium with a piece of wire mesh. You must be certain to securely place the wire

Quarantining new gerbils allows you to monitor their health and helps prevent the transmission of illness among your pets.

so that the weight of a gerbil pressing against it will not cause the mesh to fall. If the mesh gives way, the gerbils could reach each other and fight. The spaces between the wire mesh should also be small enough that a gerbil cannot push his nose through and bite the other gerbil.

Over the next several days, switch the gerbils and handfuls of bedding from each of their cages several times a day between the

Quick & Easy Gerbil Care

cages or sides of the cage. Usually the two gerbils will accept each other within several days. If they fight, you must continue switching them back and forth for several more days before once again housing them within the same cage.

Carefully watch your gerbils for the first few days they share a home to make sure that they do not fight and have accepted one another. Any wounds from bites could indicate that the two gerbils still do not like each other.

Quarantine

Serious hobbyists who breed gerbils usually quarantine a new arrival from their other gerbils, even if the newcomer seems healthy. A quarantine period helps prevent the transmission of illness among gerbils, and this is probably a good plan for all gerbil owners. Quarantine involves keeping the new arrival in a cage as far away as possible from the other animals, and the quarantine period can last from two to three weeks.

The Law and Gerbil Ownership

In some states, certain species of pets are not legal for pet stores to sell or for you to own. Although there is national legislation that governs the keeping of animals, individual states still have their own laws, and these laws vary from state to state, from county to county, and even from city to city. States can ban personal ownership of an animal species for various reasons.

In California, it is not legal to keep gerbils as pets. The California Department of Fish and Game has banned gerbils because of concerns that if gerbils become established in the wild, they could damage crops and displace native wildlife. Make sure it is legal to own a gerbil in your area before you obtain one as a pet.

During this time, the gerbil's health is monitored. When the isolation period is over, the newcomer can be moved into the area containing the other gerbils, assuming he has exhibited no signs of ill health. Pet owners rarely quarantine a new arrival, often because it means having to buy another cage and accessories. If you purchased your new gerbil from a serious breeder or a clean pet store, there is probably a low risk of any illness. Nonetheless, it is still a stressful time for both gerbils, and stress can cause gerbils to get sick. Therefore, the best approach is to always quarantine a new arrival.

Gerbils and Children

Very young children always need to be watched when they are playing with a gerbil. If a gerbil struggles while being held, some children tend to squeeze even harder instead of relaxing their hold. Sometimes this rough handling can frighten a gerbil and cause him to scratch or bite. A parent can help reduce the risk of a bite by showing children how to properly hold their gerbil and instructing them on what to do should their pet begin to wiggle and scratch (for example, return the gerbil into his cage). Children can also be told to open the cage and let the gerbil come to them rather than pulling the gerbil out of his home.

Housing
Your Gerbil

A cage is the most expensive piece of equipment you will need to buy for your gerbils, though this is generally a one-time purchase. The general rule when buying a cage is to choose the largest cage you can afford. To save money, you might be tempted to select a small cage, but it's extremely important to provide your gerbil with the largest cage possible. A cage that is too small and confining will become dirty and smelly more quickly, and it can lead to abnormal behaviors and irritable gerbils. The more room you provide your pets in which to play and explore, the more interesting and healthy they will be.

Remember, your gerbils will spend most of their lives in their cage. The cage you choose must be a comfortable, roomy home for your pets. A cage is a one-time expense that will last for the lifetime of your pets and for any future gerbils.

Cage Size

An ideal cage for a pair of gerbils measures 20 inches long by 12 inches wide by 10 inches high. You should not need to take a tape measure to the pet store. Most manufacturers label their cages for specific kinds of small pets, such as for gerbils or hamsters. These labels usually provide reasonable guidelines.

It's important to buy the largest cage you can afford so that your gerbils have plenty of room to carry out their daily activities.

If you have any doubts, always err in favor of buying a larger cage rather than a small cage. Gerbils can sometimes use the larger cages designed for hamsters and mice, but because gerbils are best kept in pairs (whereas hamsters are best kept as single pets), not all hamster cages provide adequate space for a pair of gerbils.

Gerbils need cages with enough room for separate eating, sleeping, and toilet areas. Because gerbils are not natural climbers, they do best in a cage that provides maximum floor space rather than extra height. Gerbils are not as acrobatic as some small animals, but they will enjoy a two- or three-story wire cage, especially if you provide toys for them to play with on each additional level.

Types of Cages
Metal Cages
Wire-frame cages made of galvanized steel have good ventilation and offer a good view of your gerbils. A good quality wire-frame cage should be easy to clean with a slide-out or snap-off bottom tray. It should have a large door opening with no sharp edges, or a removable top or side to provide easy access to the interior of the cage. Check that the door latches securely and cannot be easily pushed out at a corner by a persistent gerbil. The bar spacing should measure no more than one-half an inch apart to prevent young gerbils from escaping.

A gerbil's acidic urine can corrode the metal pan that fits beneath a wire cage. You can help prevent this problem by cleaning your pets' bathroom area every few days or by lining the tray bottom with foil (as long as your gerbils do not have access to the tray). Plastic trays will not corrode from urine, but some gerbils will chew on the plastic.

If you choose a wire-frame cage, try to find one with high-bottom tray sides to catch bedding and other debris that your gerbils will kick out during their normal activities. Alternatively, place the cage on top of newspaper that extends for several inches more than the cage's diameter, or you can place the cage inside a kitty litter pan to catch the material that spills out.

Aquariums

Glass aquariums provide adequate homes only for gerbils who are allowed a lot of free time outside of the cage. This is because aquarium housing is not well ventilated. Such cages are beneficial because they are not drafty, but poor ventilation and lax cleaning habits can cause ammonia gas to build up to uncomfortable levels, which can irritate your gerbils' respiratory system.

Gerbils only produce small amounts of concentrated urine, but if you decide to use an aquarium for housing, you must be extremely vigilant in keeping such a cage clean in order to protect your gerbil's health. If you can smell your pets' home, then it is certainly an unhealthy environment.

A ten-gallon or larger aquarium with a secure wire-screen cover is a good choice for housing gerbils. Because gerbils can jump right out of an aquarium, their cage must always be covered. Pet stores sell wire screens just for this purpose with latches to secure the top to the aquarium. Gerbils spend a lot of time digging and kicking shavings and food about their cage, so an aquarium will keep the area around their cage clean. Because there are no wire bars, gerbils are unlikely to injure their noses by gnawing on the bars. However,

Wooden Cages

A wooden cage is not recommended, as your pet may chew the wood and escape. In addition, wooden cages are difficult to keep clean, because they tend to absorb urine and other odors.

Quick & Easy Gerbil Care

the glass sides can become dirty and difficult to see through if not kept clean.

Gerbil Playgrounds

Colorful plastic types of housing with connecting tubes allow you to expand your gerbils' cage into a playground. However, like aquariums, this type of housing provides less ventilation than wire cages. Tube housing tends to develop offensive odors more quickly than all other types of housing, especially if not cleaned frequently enough. The plastic can also become dirty and must be regularly washed.

If you want tube housing for your gerbils, be sure to choose a large cage and select a model with maximum ventilation. Some gerbil owners combine tube housing with a wire-frame cage by cutting an opening in the wire cage and securely fitting a plastic tube into the opening. They then connect additional tubes to create a maze of tunnels for their pets. If you choose this option, be certain that there is no space between the wire and tubes that could allow your pets to escape.

Cage Accessories

Bedding

No matter what type of housing you buy, your gerbils need bedding in their cage. Bedding serves a number of purposes. Bedding is used to absorb moisture (from urine, and water from the occasional leaking water bottle), reduce odors, and provide a warm, dry place for your pet to sleep. Bedding also allows gerbils to engage in some natural behaviors, such as burrowing and building a sleeping nest.

Pet stores carry a variety of small animal beddings that are suitable for gerbils, including wood shavings (such as pine, aspen, or pine treated with chlorophyll for odor control), and more sophisticated beddings made from recycled paper or wood pulp that are designed to help control or eliminate odor. The latter types are more expensive, but they can make it more pleasurable to own gerbils because their home will be less likely to smell unpleasant between cage cleanings.

Bedding made from recycled paper also contains no harmful inks, dyes, or significant levels of heavy metals, and because most newspaper inks are now vegetable-based, not petroleum-based, they are not harmful to small animals such as gerbils. Whatever bedding you choose, provide a deep layer, about four inches, inside your gerbils' cage so they can dig and burrow.

Bedding is an important component of your gerbils' environment and it can affect their health. Ideally, small animal bedding should be dust-free. Dusty bedding can irritate a gerbil's respiratory system or aggravate an existing respiratory ailment. Because gerbils are housed directly on their bedding and happily burrow and dig through the bedding, they are more likely to stir up fine particles and be at risk for these potential problems. In general, paper pulp and recycled paper products tend to be lower in dust compared to

Safe Bedding

 Do not use corncob or cat litter for your pets' bedding. These coarse materials are abrasive—when gerbils dig and burrow in these coarse types of bedding, it can sometimes cut their faces.

Cage Accessories

Your gerbil will need the following cage accessories. Many different varieties are sold at your local pet shop.

- Food dishes
- Hanging water bottle
- Nesting box
- Bedding material
- Toys

wood shavings. Peat moss is sometimes suggested as bedding for gerbils, but it can be very dusty and is not recommended.

Odor Control

While some types of bedding contain odor-masking agents, such as chlorophyll in shavings, the development of innovative bedding products has been spurred in part by the quest to control or eliminate odor. Scientifically developed bedding products made from a variety of materials, such as recycled paper, do not just mask odor; they are designed to reduce odor by controlling the formation of ammonia. Such beddings promote a healthier environment for gerbils compared with traditional beddings.

When deciding which bedding to use, take into account your gerbils' cage type. If it is a well-ventilated wire cage, the necessity of using the more expensive bedding is reduced. However, if your gerbils are housed in an aquarium or family members complain about the smell of your gerbils, such bedding is highly recommended. Remember, unless cage cleaning is neglected, gerbils do not typically smell bad.

The Cedar Shavings Controversy

Shavings made from softwoods, which include pine and cedar, are

Nesting Suggestions

Place your gerbils' food dish, water bottle, and nest box at one end of their cage. This will help your gerbils establish a bathroom area away from their sleeping and eating areas.

still the most common type of bedding for small pets such as gerbils. These beddings have been popular because they are relatively inexpensive and are often fragrant smelling, particularly cedar shavings. The pleasant smell associated with these materials is due to the aromatic compounds found in the wood.

However, cedar shavings have been implicated as both causing and aggravating respiratory problems in small animals. In addition, they are known to affect liver function in rats and mice. However, few controlled scientific studies have documented these problems. More common are reports that when an animal was removed from cedar shavings, the symptoms of poor health (such as breathing distress) disappeared. Although not all experts agree that cedar shavings present a risk to small pets, a growing body of evidence seems to support hobbyists' contentions that cedar shavings can have an

Nesting Material

It's a good idea to give your gerbils unscented tissue paper or paper towels to shred into nesting material. Pet stores also sell nesting material that you can use. However, do not buy artificial fiber bedding sold for birds and hamsters. The small fibers can wrap around a gerbil's feet and cut off circulation, and sometimes gerbils eat this material and cannot pass it out of their system.

Quick & Easy Gerbil Care

adverse effect on small animals. Therefore, cedar shavings are not recommended for your gerbils.

Food Dishes

You will need at least two sets of dishes for your gerbils' food. This way you will have one that can be in use while the other is being cleaned. Ceramic crock-style dishes or stainless steel dishes are the best materials because they are easy to clean, sturdy, and made of a heavy material. If you have a metal cage, you can attach the dish to the side to prevent your pets from tipping it over and spilling the contents. If you use a freestanding dish, make sure it is heavy enough that your gerbils cannot tip it over. Pet stores sell a variety of colorful ceramic dishes that are too heavy for a gerbil to move.

Round, crock-style food dishes made of stainless steel or ceramic are the most sturdy and easy to clean.

There are many types of nesting boxes you can provide for your gerbils, including cardboard tunnels, plastic houses, or even old cereal boxes or milk cartons.

The Water Bottle

The best way to provide your gerbils with fresh water is to use a gravity-fed water bottle sold at pet stores. A special holder, also available at pet stores, enables you to hang the water bottle in an aquarium if you are using that type of housing. Do not use an open dish to provide your gerbils with water. While digging and playing in their cage, your gerbils will kick bedding and food into the water, which will become unsanitary. Furthermore, the increased moisture from a spilled dish of water can create an unhealthy, damp environment, especially in an aquarium-type cage. In case the bottle leaks, do not place it over your pets' food dish.

Nesting Box

Gerbils need a nesting box for sleeping and security. This

"bedroom" gives gerbils a safe place where they can hide from loud noises and any disturbing activity outside of their cage. You can buy a nesting box at a pet store. A variety of types are sold, including ones that are made to satisfy a small animal's natural instinct to chew, such as fruit-flavored cardboard tunnels, huts made from natural plant fibers, and wooden blocks that a pet hollows out. Other kinds are less destructible and are made of ceramic or hard plastic. You can also make your pets a nest box from an old cereal box or milk carton. Once the box becomes chewed up or smelly, you will need to replace it.

Toys

The greater the variety of toys, the more fun your gerbils will have, and the more fun they are to watch. Toys are also beneficial to your gerbils' health because by providing your gerbils with a variety of toys on which to play and explore, you help reduce the likelihood of their becoming overweight. Give your gerbils toys designed for hamsters and mice, such as wood chew sticks, tunnels, and ladders. Many wooden toys made for parakeets and parrots are safe to use with your gerbils. Wood chews keep gerbils busy and active and provide a hard surface for them to gnaw, which helps to keep their teeth in good shape.

However, do not overcrowd your gerbils' cage with toys. This leaves little room for the gerbils, and your pets might be injured

Make Your Own Toys

Most gerbils will enjoy playing with almost anything you put in their cage. Some favorite homemade toys are cardboard rolls from empty toilet paper or paper towels. You can partially bury these tubes under your gerbils' bedding and create a system of tunnels for them to explore. Be creative and connect multiple rolls and make multiple entrances and exits.

accidentally if a toy falls on them. Alternating toys is a trick that dog and cat owners have used for years, and gerbil owners can use this trick as well. Let your gerbils play with a toy for a week, then take it away and replace it with a new toy. The following week you can temporarily take away the new toy and replace it with the old one. By switching your pets' toys around, your gerbils will stay active and interested in exploring their environment. Gerbils will chew on whatever you put in their cage, so be sure the toys are safe.

Exercise wheels are toys that most gerbils seem to love. However, it is recommended that you purchase a solid-floor exercise wheel without side spokes because your gerbil's leg or tail can easily get caught in the sides. Solid-floor exercise wheels are commonly sold in pet stores, or they can be specially ordered.

Cage Placement

Your gerbils should be part of your family. Place their cage in a location where you can watch and enjoy them. Make the cage a pleasant part of the room, and it's best to set up the cage on a dresser or table with some attractive fabric beneath it. The floor is not the most ideal location, as the temperature near the floor is often cooler than on a dresser or table. Your gerbils' cage should be placed out of the view of the family cat and dog.

Do not keep your pets in the garage. Not only is it unhealthy from automobile exhaust, but the temperature is also more extreme and variable and your pets are more likely to be neglected. Also, do not place your pets' cage near a heating or air conditioning vent, a drafty window, or in direct sunlight. Gerbils are easily susceptible to overheating, chills, and drafts. Gerbils can tolerate a house's normal variations in room temperature, light, and humidity, although ideal conditions consist of 60°F to 70°F with a maximum relative humidity of 30 to 50 percent. Gerbils must be kept in a dry environment. Gerbils that live in homes or cages with an environmental humidity greater than 50 percent will be

Exercise wheels are the favorite toys of most gerbils, and they can be found in pet stores everywhere.

stressed and their fur will stand out and appear matted instead of lying smoothly.

Cage Cleaning

A clean cage plays an important role in keeping your gerbils healthy. No matter how much a gerbil grooms himself, if the cage is dirty, the gerbil will not be able to keep himself smelling clean. A gerbil's cage will smell only if it is not cleaned often enough. Therefore, it's best to clean the cage at least once a week. The more gerbils kept in a cage, especially in a cage that is too small, the more often the cage will have to be cleaned.

Like other small pets, many gerbils will use a corner of their cage for a bathroom. Therefore, you need to replace the bedding in this area. A complete change of bedding once a week is the only way to provide your naturally tidy pets with the clean home they desire.

Housing Your Gerbil

Quick Cleaning Tip

Instead of feeling overwhelmed with the daunting task of a thorough cleaning and thus postponing it, try using a kitty litter scoop to quickly remove and replace some of the soiled bedding. Doing so can allow the cage to remain sanitary a few extra days before you undertake a more meticulous cleaning. Another way to make cage cleaning easier is to buy larger quantities of bedding so you always have some around for a quick change.

Once a month, do a thorough cleaning. If necessary, disinfect the cage and the surrounding area. Pet stores sell mild cleansers that are safe for animals. Wash the cage with warm soapy water. Be sure to rinse and dry it thoroughly. Wash the water bottle, food dish, and any plastic toys. Wood toys can eventually splinter if washed in water, but scraping them clean with a file is effective. Scrape or file off any grime that might have accumulated on the bars of a wire cage. Replace the nest box as needed. If you play with your pets while you clean their home, cage cleaning will not be a dreary chore. You can also let them run around in a run-about-ball (one gerbil per ball!) while you clean.

Feeding Your Gerbil

Gerbils are herbivorous, which means they eat green plants, seeds, fruits, berries, grains, and nuts. Some gerbils like to snack on an occasional invertebrate, such as live mealworms, which are sold at pet stores, and in the wild, gerbils eat whatever they come across while foraging, such as seeds, grains, and an occasional spider or beetle. However, the Mongolian gerbil is still considered to be a herbivore.

Nutrition is a key factor in promoting good health and a long life. Feeding your gerbils a healthy diet is also very easy to do because a variety of commercial foods are sold for gerbils at pet stores. These foods are typically sold in packages marked for both hamsters and gerbils. The dietary requirements for hamsters and gerbils are similar, and foods sold for hamsters can usually be fed safely to gerbils.

A balanced diet for gerbils includes the appropriate amounts of protein, carbohydrate, fat, vitamins, and minerals. All these nutrients interact in the building, maintenance, and functioning of a gerbil's body. It is also important to feed a diet that does not contain too much of these nutrients.

Fortunately, because gerbils have been used in scientific research, much reliable information exists on their nutritional needs. The amount of protein your pets need is influenced by a number of physiological factors, including age. Gerbils need less protein when they are adults than they do when they are growing, pregnant, or nursing a litter of babies. A good diet for gerbils should contain approximately 18 to 22 percent protein.

Gerbils are herbivorous, which means they eat green plants, seeds, nuts, and berries—though some wild gerbils occasionally eat small insects.

Nuts to Gerbils

Gerbils love nuts, especially the sunflower seeds that are in mixes of gerbil food. However, because nuts are fatty, too many nuts will cause a gerbil to become overweight and susceptible to a variety of other health problems, including bone fractures, problems with bone development, growth problems, and a shorter lifespan. Therefore, only feed nuts on occasion as a treat, and make sure your gerbil is getting enough healthy foods.

Carbohydrates are used as a source of energy. Your gerbils will easily get enough carbohydrates with a diet based on seeds and grains. Most seeds and grains are at least 50 percent carbohydrate.

Seeds

A good base diet for your gerbil is one of the gerbil and hamster mixes sold at pet stores. These mixes contain seeds, grains, nuts, alfalfa pellets, and sometimes dry kibble. Packaged foods for gerbils typically contain all the nutrients your pets need to remain healthy. Do not choose a food that consists predominately of sunflower seeds or other nuts.

You will find that your pets have a preference for certain items in the mix, such as the sunflower seeds, and will not eat others, such as the

Fats

Fats are a significant source of calories and energy. They make up part of the structure of every cell and are necessary for absorption of fat-soluble vitamins, including vitamins A, D, and E. Fats help to prevent and alleviate skin problems. However, fats must be fed in moderation.

Hand-Feeding

If your pets are housed in a wire cage, do not feed them through the cage bars. Otherwise, anything (including a finger) that is poked through the cage bars might get nipped. Always open the cage door to offer a treat. In addition, wash your hands before handling your gerbils in case any food smells on your hands entice your gerbil to nip.

alfalfa pellets. Over time, this "selective feeding" can cause inadequate nutrition and problems of obesity and bone fractures. Because a food's nutritional analysis is based on consumption of the entire mix of ingredients, a selective eater may not be getting a nutritious, complete diet. Nutrient deficiencies can take some time before they appear. While it is reasonable not to expect your gerbils to like some items in their food, consistently refusing to eat more than half of a food's ingredients is not healthy.

You can combat a gerbil's tendency toward selective eating in several ways. Try offering a different brand of gerbil food, as it might contain a more palatable blend of ingredients. Consider also feeding nutritionally complete pellets or laboratory blocks manufactured specifically for gerbils and hamsters.

Pellets

Pellets are a great base diet for gerbils. The ingredients in these blocks are blended so that a gerbil cannot pick out one ingredient, and he will, therefore, consume adequate nutrients. The texture of the blocks can influence how much your gerbils eat. The pellets and blocks are hard and help to keep a gerbil's teeth trim. However, during cold, dry weather, the pellets and blocks can become very hard, making them difficult for young gerbils to eat. During damp, humid weather they may become soft. Stale pellets and blocks, which might be crumbly or soft, are not only less nutritious, but they are also less palatable to gerbils.

Fruits and Vegetables

In addition to pellets and/or the gerbil mix of grains and seeds, you should feed your pets a mixture of fresh fruits and vegetables. Gerbils relish fresh fruits and vegetables and should be given daily treats of small, well-washed pieces of vegetables and fruits. However, too much of these foods could cause gut ache or diarrhea.

Look at your gerbils' front paws and use the size of their hands as a reasonable guide when deciding how much of a fresh food item to offer your pets. A gerbil should be able to easily hold a piece of the diced fruit or vegetable between his hands. Leafy greens should be no more than about one inch by one inch in size. By using this conservative estimate of the amount, your pets are less likely to experience any problems.

Start off by offering your pets only one fresh item a day. You can slowly increase the amount to two or three pieces per day. The amount should depend on the type of food and whether your ger-

Hoarding

Pay attention when feeding your gerbils their fresh food. Some gerbils will cart off and hide a piece of vegetable or fruit in their nest. If the gerbil does not eat the food right away, it could spoil. Every day, you will need to remove any uneaten fresh foods before offering your pets additional items.

If there are constantly leftover fresh foods, you are probably feeding your gerbils too much and should reduce the amount you feed. Ideally, you want your gerbils to consume fresh foods right away.

bils have eaten it before. Offer previously untried foods in very small pieces to make sure your gerbils like it and to make sure it will not cause digestive upset (evidenced by diarrhea).

Moist foods, like cucumbers and lettuce, should be fed only in very small amounts. Gerbils enjoy healthy vegetables such as carrots, broccoli, cauliflower, cabbage, peas, tomatoes, beets, celery, red peppers, avocados, and fruits such as apples, bananas, apricots, peaches, plums, and berries. Gerbils will also relish fresh dandelion greens, including the yellow flowers. If you opt to feed your pets dandelions, make sure you obtain them from a location free of pesticides and herbicides. Wash and dry them as you would with lettuce, and offer only a small piece each day.

Treats

Treats can be offered to your gerbils on occasion. Some gerbils like to nibble hay cubes or loose hay. Because the hay is dried, its moisture content is much lower, and it can be fed to your gerbils quite often. Look for hay products in the rabbit section of a pet store.

Fresh fruits and vegetables should be included in your gerbils' everyday diet.

Unhealthy Treats

While it can be fun to offer your gerbils new types of food and see if they enjoy them, not all foods are suitable for gerbils. What shouldn't you feed your gerbils? Do not feed them dry cat food, which is too high in protein. Seed and nut mixes sold for parrots and cockatiels should also be avoided due to the high fat content of the nuts.

Do not feed your gerbils junk food made for people. Although gerbils will greedily eat potato chips and eagerly look for more, potato chips, cookies, candy, and other snack foods are not healthy for your pets.

Pet stores also sell a variety of delectable treats just for gerbils. Again, moderation is the key when feeding your gerbils treats. Your gerbils should not eat so many treats that they have no appetite for their regular food.

Other treats to try offering your gerbils include dry, unsweetened cereals. Gerbils also enjoy pretzels, crackers, stale bread, hard uncooked noodles, uncooked rice, and uncooked hot cereals (for example, cracked four-grain cereal). Many gerbils love dog biscuits, but be cautious when offering any of your dog's regular kibble, as some brands are too high in fat. These treats, as well as the hard foods in your gerbils' regular diet, will help to keep their teeth trim.

Some live foods can also be given as treats. Gerbils do enjoy chasing, catching, and eating live mealworms and crickets. Both crickets and mealworms are sold at pet stores for reptiles. However, feed live foods as a treat, only one or two every few days.

Vitamins

Vitamins are necessary as catalysts for chemical reactions in the body. A number of vitamins, such as vitamin B, are synthesized in gerbils by intestinal bacteria. These vitamins are available to gerbils

Vitamin Supplements

by means of coprophagy: the eating of special droppings that contain the vitamins synthesized by the bacteria. Therefore, do not be concerned if you see your pets engaged in such behavior, as coprophagy is necessary for their good health.

Gerbils require minerals and trace elements, such as iron, calcium, phosphate, and iodine. Minerals have many functions, from the structural role of calcium and phosphate in bones to the role of iron in bringing oxygen to the body. You can see what percentage of minerals is contained in some commercial gerbil foods by looking at the percentage of ash (ash is primarily minerals) listed under the guaranteed analysis. However, the percentage does not tell you exactly what minerals are present or in what amounts. Feeding your gerbils a fresh, high-quality diet will usually ensure adequate intake of need vitamins and minerals.

A Total Feeding Plan
How Much to Feed
How much your gerbils need to eat will change throughout their lives. The amount will vary according to your gerbils' age, gender, and activity level. Young, growing gerbils will need to eat more food per gram of body weight than do adults. Because male gerbils are larger than females, they need to eat more food than do females. Gerbils that are allowed to run around and play outside their cage frequently will require more food than gerbils that spend a lot of time in their cage.

When to Feed

It is best to feed your gerbils the same amount of food at the same time each day. Because gerbils are active during both the day and night, you can select a feeding time that best suits your schedule. Many pet owners prefer to feed their gerbils when they come home from school or work.

Your gerbils will begin to anticipate feeding time and become more active while waiting for their food. Each day, you will need to discard the old food in their dish and replace it with fresh food. The obvious satisfaction and delight that gerbils take when sorting through a fresh dish of food makes feeding a rewarding time to observe your pets. Watching your pets eat, even for a few minutes, will help you determine that they are both active and well.

Adjusting the Amount of Food Served

Because gerbils like to nibble on food throughout the day and night, be sure your pets always have food in their dish. If your gerbils' dish is empty, increase the amount of food you feed your pets. A gerbil will eat about a tablespoonful of food a day, but the amount will vary depending on what type of food you feed and how active your gerbils are. You should adjust the amount of food you offer based on your observations.

You want to feed each gerbil enough food to maintain a stable weight. Your gerbils should feel solid and sleek without any extra padding on their sides from fat. Any marked loss or increase in a gerbil's appetite could signal illness.

Fresh is Best

It is important that the food is fresh. Food that is old can become stale and lose some of its nutritional value. Packaged foods should be fresh and sweet smelling, not rancid or dusty. Some manufacturers stamp a date on food bags and recommend that the food be used within one year of this date. Do not buy large quantities of food because it will take too long a time to use all of it.

Proper storage of your gerbils' food is essential. Store your gerbils' food in a cool, dry environment. Exposure to sunlight, heat, and time degrade the vitamins in a food. Therefore, keep your gerbils' food in an airtight container, such as a glass jar with a lid, or be sure to completely close a container that is self-sealing. This will keep the food fresh and prevent it from spoiling.

Water

Gerbils conserve water by concentrating their urine, an adaptation to their original desert home. Compared with other small animals, gerbils consume comparatively little water. Because of their smaller size (an average of 70 grams), female gerbils consume between 2.8 to 5.7 milliliters of water a day compared to the 3.3 to 5.7 milliliters that males drink each day.

At least once a week, change the water in your gerbils' water bottle. Because they drink so little water, some pet owners neglect this task, figuring the water is still fresh. However, the water can become distasteful and contaminated with bacteria and other harmful pathogens. Use a slender bristle brush to clean the slimy residue that will coat the bottle. Check to see that the stopper is not clogged with bedding.

Some gerbils nibble the metal waterspout. Check to be sure there are no jagged ends that could cut your pets. If there are, you will need to replace the water bottle.

Taming and Activities for Your Gerbil

Part of the fun of owning gerbils is taking them out of their cage to play. The more you play with your gerbils and let them explore, the happier they will be. However, before you let your gerbils out to play, it is a good idea to hand-tame them. A tame gerbil will let you hold and pick him up without becoming frightened. The more time you spend holding and playing with your gerbils, the more quickly they will learn to trust you.

How to Hand-Tame Your Gerbil

Before you can regularly pick up your gerbils, you need to make sure that they are comfortable with the presence of your hand and

Treats can be a helpful aid in hand-taming your gerbils.

that they understand that you are not a threat. This is called hand-taming.

The first step in taming your gerbils is to let them sniff and crawl on your hand. Place a food treat in the palm of your hand and encourage them to climb onto your hand. Do not make rapid movements with your hands. Slowly move them and occasionally use a finger to pet a gerbil along his side, head, or tail. Even a brief, momentary stroke will work.

Continue to slowly pet your gerbils within their cage under a variety of conditions and times. Eventually your pets will hop into your hands. They might even climb out of the cage and up your arm. Replace the gerbils in their home before they get too far up your arm and they will renew their quest to explore outside their cage with vigor and confidence.

How to Correctly Hold a Gerbil
Once your gerbils are hand-tamed and are no longer afraid of being

handled by you, you can begin picking them up and holding them. It is important to pick up gerbils carefully and gently so that you do not hurt them.

Pick up one gerbil at a time by letting him climb onto your hand or by scooping him up under his belly. Gerbils can be frightened when a hand descends down over their backs, so always put your hand in their cage palm up, lower it to the bottom of the cage, and then move it toward your gerbil. Practice picking up each gerbil in the cage before taking him out.

Gerbils are nimble and will often try to get away, so hold the base of your pet's tail (not the tip!) with one hand and cradle his body in the palm of your hand. Do not turn him over on his back and expose his belly. This posture makes gerbils (and most animals) feel vulnerable, and they will become upset and will struggle frantically to right themselves. Keep in mind that a normally docile gerbil might bite you when he is in pain or is frightened.

Always use two hands when holding your gerbil, and support his body so that he feels secure.

Taming and Activities for Your Gerbil   47

When you hold your gerbil, always use two hands. Gerbils are prone to bouts of inspiration that can cause some to leap out of your hands. For this reason, one hand should support your gerbil's body while your other hand is cupped over his back. Snuggle your gerbil against your body for greater security. It is also prudent to immediately sit on the ground when first teaching a gerbil to be held. Then, if he does jump, the distance is much less than if you were standing.

Gerbil Body Language

Knowing your gerbils' body language can help you be more sensitive to your pets' moods and help you to tame them better. You do not want to continue playing with your pets if they become scared. When frightened, your pets might run away, kick, bite, or scratch. When nervous, gerbils sit stiffly with their front paws held tightly in front of their chest. As part of the "flight or fight response," some frightened gerbils defecate. If your pets exhibit any of these behaviors, you should talk gently to them, then put them back into their cage so that they can calm down.

During both play and fight, gerbils often push at each other with their front paws. Preceding a fight, their tails often bend stiffly up instead of lying on the ground. When they are happy, some gerbils

Recapturing a Loose Gerbil

Should your gerbil escape from his home (or become lost while exploring outside his cage), place the cage on the floor where your pet always begins his exploration. Do not leave the cage door open because the other gerbil will join the wanderer. Instead, provide that gerbil with a new nest box, take the old nest box along with the nesting material, and place it on the floor outside but next to the cage. Quite often, the gerbil will return to the cage area and then fall asleep inside his familiar nest box.

Quick & Easy Gerbil Care

The Fragile Tail

Don't pick up a gerbil by his tail. For one thing, the gerbil can turn and bite your finger, which will probably cause you to drop him. For another thing, the skin on the gerbil's tail will come off. The tail will eventually atrophy and fall off or a veterinarian will need to amputate the tail. A gerbil can live without his tail, but careful handling on your part will prevent tail loss from ever happening.

spring and leap in the air. You might also hear your pets softly grinding their teeth together when they are happy. When curious, gerbils will stand up on their hind legs, ears alert, and noses twitching to investigate their surroundings.

If your gerbils are sleeping when you want to play with them, call their names, tap on their nest box, and allow them a few moments to wake up before you visit. Forcing them to come out of their nest box when they would clearly rather sleep is not a good way to start taming your pets.

Fun Activities for Your Gerbil

Many people allow their pets to explore and play in the room in which their cage is kept. Before doing this, you must "gerbil-proof" the room. Pick up "edible" items off the floor. Gerbils can eat and dig up potted plants and can chew electrical cords, papers, and books. Close up nooks and crannies so that your gerbils do not escape.

Place your pets' cage on the floor and let them begin their exploration from their home. Your pets' cage is their refuge and gives them a sense of security and safety. Should your gerbils become scared, they can quickly run back into their cage. If your gerbils live in an aquarium, use a bird ladder to let your pets easily get in and out of their cage.

Run-About-Balls

One way to allow your gerbils to safely play outside their cage is to set up a large plastic enclosure made especially for small pets. Gerbil owners set these up much like a child's playpen. Plastic run-about-balls are another fun option. Only one gerbil can be placed in a run-about-ball at a time. Supervise your pets when they are in the run-about-balls. Stairs and other pets are potential hazards. Some balls are designed to move on a racetrack, which helps to confine your gerbils' movements to a safe place.

Supervising Playtime

Never let your pets loose in a room without supervising them. Watch them closely so they do not chew items or become "lost" by finding a secret cubbyhole for a new sleeping nest. Also be aware that your gerbils might leave droppings in the room as they explore. Gerbils cannot be housebroken.

If you want your pets to return to their cage, but they still want to explore, do not chase after them. Doing so will surely scare them and will prolong the time it will take to entice them back into their cage. Gerbils can run fast and may be difficult to catch. Most loose gerbils, however, will explore a room and will not hide. They will return to their cage or your hand if tempted by a treat.

To encourage your pets to re-enter their home, try placing fresh-smelling treats of fruit or vegetables in their food dish. Unlike pet rats, gerbils are not readily taught to come when called by their name.

Gerbil Health Care

When purchased from a reliable source and given good care, gerbils are hardy and resilient. In fact, gerbils do not appear to be prone to as many potential ailments as other small pets, such as mice and hamsters.

You will learn how your pets behave when they are frightened or excited, how they react to new situations, and what it means when they assume different postures. Knowing a gerbil's normal behavior will help you recognize when one of your pets might be sick. Any changes in behavior, such as lack of interest in playing or eating, could mean your gerbil is ill and you should consult a veterinarian.

Don't Play Vet

If one of your gerbils is displaying signs of illness or just doesn't seem to be acting like his normal frisky self, take him to the veterinarian for a checkup. Only your vet should diagnose any medical problem your gerbils may be experiencing.

Finding a Veterinarian

In order for your gerbil to receive the proper treatment, he needs the correct diagnosis. A veterinarian who routinely treats rodents and has a special interest in their care is best qualified and will most likely have the necessary, smaller-sized equipment. In order to locate a veterinarian who is knowledgeable about rodents, inquire at pet stores, critter clubs, rescue societies, and also at veterinarians' offices.

Even when you recognize that your gerbil might be "under the weather," you might hesitate to take your pet to a veterinarian due to the potential expense. A visit to a veterinarian can be expensive and it can be difficult to spend large sums of money on such a visit. Discuss potential costs with your veterinarian beforehand, so that you will have a better idea how much your gerbil's care might cost.

How to Recognize a Sick Pet

As you gain experience caring for your gerbils, you will also become more proficient in recognizing when your pets are sick. Sick gerbils generally present a similar range of symptoms. Obvious signs of illness include discharge from the eyes or nose. Because they are fastidious and keep themselves clean, the discharge is often visible on their paws from their grooming efforts. Sudden changes in behavior, such as lethargy and reduced appetite, can also indicate illness.

Quick & Easy Gerbil Care

Quick Action

Most small pets that are sick need to be immediately treated by a veterinarian. This is especially important because pet owners often do not notice symptoms in their pet until the animal is very ill. By the time a pet owner realizes that his or her animal is ill, the pet has usually been sick for quite some time. Furthermore, keep in mind that the sicker a gerbil is, the more likely he is to be traumatized from the procedures at a veterinarian's office.

Signs of disease are more difficult to detect but include rough hair, hunched posture, and weight loss. You should pay particular attention if your gerbil is sensitive when touched on certain part of his body, as this could indicate an injury.

Any of these symptoms suggest that something might be wrong with your gerbil and a visit to the veterinarian might be prudent. This is especially important because you are unlikely to notice symptoms in your gerbil until he is very ill. By the time you realize your gerbil is ill, your pet may have been sick for quite some time. In many cases, treatment is difficult because the condition is so advanced at the time of detection.

Signs of Illness in a Gerbil

If your gerbil shows any of the following signs, he might be ill. Take him to a veterinarian as soon as possible.

- Not eating or drinking
- Lethargy
- Runny nose, weepy eyes
- Diarrhea
- Failure to groom himself
- Weight loss

Common Gerbil Ailments

The ailments that might affect gerbils can be classified into six categories: (1) trauma-induced injuries and illness, (2) infectious diseases, (3) noninfectious diseases, (4) improper husbandry, (5) heredity, and (6) aging. The reasons that a gerbil becomes sick are often a combination of factors from more than one category. Numerous factors affect how sick the gerbil will get. These factors include the virulence of the pathogen, the gerbil's age, dietary deficiencies, and whether the gerbil is already sick with another illness.

Trauma-Induced Injuries and Illness

When a gerbil has a traumatic injury, it is usually obvious. The gerbil is often in acute and immediate pain and distress. Trauma can be easier to treat than infectious diseases because it is easier to detect. If a gerbil is injured, you should bring him to a veterinarian right away. Sometimes, certain trauma injuries (such as injured toes) get better despite no care. Broken bones are a potential hazard because gerbils are wiggly and jump.

Fighting Injuries

Injuries from fighting between gerbils can sometimes occur. Occasionally, an established pair of gerbils becomes aggressive and

Watch for Wounds

Injuries from fighting among gerbils can sometimes occur. Because infection is always possible when a gerbil is bitten in a fight, clean any bloody injuries with warm water and an antiseptic or hydrogen peroxide. An abscess can develop at the site of a bite would due to bacterial infection. Watch the wounds, and if you detect any prolonged swelling or sign of redness, take your gerbil to the veterinarian.

Keeping your gerbil in a safe environment with plenty of toys to keep him occupied will help prevent stress.

fights. If you are present while the gerbils are fighting, use a towel or glove to separate them. You will probably need to keep them in separate cages.

Because infection from bacteria is always possible when an animal is bitten in a fight, clean any large bloody injuries with warm water and an antiseptic. Watch the wounds, and if you detect any prolonged swelling, take your gerbil to the veterinarian.

Stress

What is stress? Stress is a catchall word for a variety of conditions that disturb or interfere with a pet's normal physiological equilibrium. Because stress often leads to illness, it is frequently mentioned as a detrimental, contributing factor to various diseases.

Besides becoming sick, a gerbil can exhibit signs of stress in other ways, such as irritability, lack of appetite, hair loss, and loose droppings. It is useful for pet owners to be aware of what constitutes stress for their gerbils.

Gerbil Health Care

Emergency Symptoms

If your gerbil displays any of the following signs of illness, immediate veterinarian attention is needed:

- Refusing to eat or drink
- Runny nose
- Congestion
- Labored breathing
- Reluctance to move
- Paralysis
- Appearance of being in pain when handled
- Inability to defecate
- Diarrhea

A gerbil can experience stress from pain and fear, when moving to a new cage, from a change in diet, exposure to temperature fluctuations, and/or an environmental humidity that is too high. The trip from a pet store or breeder to a new home can also be frightening and stressful for gerbils. Once in their new home, some gerbils settle down right away, while others take longer to adjust.

Other stressful situations include loud noises, changes in diet, overcrowding, and harassment. Groups of gerbils housed together can fight and injure each other. Fighting and bullying is particularly stressful for the animal that is always picked on because he is at the bottom of the pecking order. Stress can be a major factor in the development of what might otherwise remain a dormant disease. Therefore, it is wise to minimize the stress in your gerbils' lives.

Abscess

An abscess is usually due to a secondary bacterial infection from a wound inflicted during a fight, or it could be caused by an infection from a cut. An abscess can develop at the site of a bite wound due to bacterial infection.

A veterinarian must tend to an abscess. Using a needle, the veterinarian will biopsy (or sample) the abscess, then drain and clean the site. Usually topical antibiotics are applied to the area.

The bacteria that cause an abscess are often opportunistic and can infect other organs besides the skin. It is important that an affected pet be properly treated. A veterinarian might deem it necessary to culture, or grow, a sample of the fluid to identify the type of bacteria present. An antibiotic selected according to cultures and sensitivity test results is likely to be highly effective.

Infectious Diseases

Infectious diseases can spread from one animal to another and are caused by bacteria, viruses, and protozoa. Sometimes the signs of infection are difficult to detect. Individual animals also differ in their resistance to infectious organisms. Some exposed animals

Diseases, such as Tyzzer's Disease, are rare in gerbils that are well cared for.

never display any symptoms. However, stress or other bacterial or viral infections can cause an animal to suddenly show symptoms.

A single pet is less at risk for infectious diseases compared to a pet that is housed in close proximity to large numbers of other animals of the same species. Infectious diseases are often preventable through good husbandry.

Tyzzer's Disease

This is a highly contagious disease that is caused by bacteria (*Clostridium piliforme*). The disease is usually fatal. Symptoms include a scruffy coat, lack of activity, diarrhea, and dehydration, although some gerbils have no obvious signs before death. Sudden death or death after a short period of illness is often the only way to diagnose this disease.

If one of your gerbils exhibits the symptoms of this disease, immediately separate the healthy gerbil from the sick gerbil. Place the sick gerbil in a covered carrying cage and take him to your veterinarian. Treatment with the appropriate antibiotics can sometimes save the sick gerbil.

If your veterinarian suspects Tyzzer's disease, antibiotics will be provided for both of your pets. Poor husbandry and stress are implicated in this disease. Prevention is easier than treatment, and this disease is rare in well-cared-for gerbils.

Noninfectious Diseases and Ailments

Noninfectious diseases and other ailments are caused by common, everyday factors. Usually, they are not life-threatening ailments but still should be evaluated and treated by a veterinarian. The following are some common noninfectious ailments.

Skin and Fur Problems

Gerbils often have skin problems. Hair loss, bloody secretions, and moist, infected skin on the muzzle and nose of gerbils are often due to infection from bacteria. This condition is called Staph dermatitis or sore nose. This disease is caused by an increase in secretions from the harderian gland and is complicated by infection with Staph bacteria.

The harderian gland produces a reddish lubricating fluid in a gerbil's eyes; the fluid then drains into his nose. It is believed that the secretions are irritating to the gerbil's skin, which then becomes infected with the bacteria. Excessive secretion is associated with stress.

Muzzle Dermatitis

Muzzle dermatitis is another condition that looks similar to Staph dermatitis. The loss of hair from the gerbil's muzzle can also be caused from mange mites or from self-inflicted trauma. The latter occurs when the gerbil constantly rubs his nose on feeders or on the cage. Housing your pet on coarse bedding, such as corncobs, has also been known to cause this condition. Your veterinarian is best qualified to diagnose and treat skin conditions in your gerbil.

Tumors

Tumors, which are a form of cancer, are a noninfectious disease. They are seldom seen in young gerbils. More often, tumors occur in middle-aged and older gerbils. When playing with your pet, you might notice a swelling under the skin, which could be a tumor or abscess. If your gerbil has a lump, you should consult a veterinarian to determine whether it is a tumor and whether surgery is needed.

Both male and female gerbils have a large scent gland in the middle of their belly. The gland is used for marking their territory. This normal gland is sometimes mistaken for a tumor. However, in old gerbils, the gland may become infected or cancerous. If you notice any changes in the size or shape of this gland, take your gerbil to the veterinarian for an examination.

Signs of Dental Problems

- Reduced food intake
- Difficulty eating
- Weight loss
- Poor coat condition
- Inability to close jaw
- Excessive salivation (slobbers)
- Nasal or eye discharge

Tooth Problems

Gerbils, like all rodents, have chisel-like incisors in the front of their mouths. These teeth never stop growing. The incisor teeth enable a gerbil to carry nuts and other food items and to easily open hard seeds and nuts. The incisors are worn down by the animal's gnawing and chewing on hard substances.

Although the condition is not common, the teeth of some gerbils need veterinary attention due to malocclusion. Malocclusion occurs when the gerbil's incisor teeth do not meet properly, either because the teeth are overgrown or they are misaligned.

A gerbil's teeth can fail to meet and wear properly for several reasons. Malocclusion can be inherited, or it can be caused by trauma, infection, or improper diet (for example, the gerbil does not regularly eat foods hard enough to wear down his teeth). Even if you inspected the gerbil's teeth before buying him, be aware that hereditary malocclusion is often not detectable in young gerbils. Even if the teeth appear normal at first, as the gerbil grows, the teeth become misaligned.

Gerbils with this condition eventually cannot eat, lose weight, and will die without treatment. Many show symptoms often referred to as "slobbers," which are threads of saliva around the mouth and sometimes wiped on the front paws. If you notice that your pet is

Quick & Easy Gerbil Care

not eating, you can check his incisors by pulling back his lips. An affected gerbil should be taken to a veterinarian who will clip or file the gerbil's teeth.

Ear Problems

Gerbils rarely get ear mites or ear infections. However, if left untreated, ear mite infestations can cause serious problems. Take your pet to a veterinarian if you notice excessive scratching, heavy wax buildup, discharge, or a growth.

The most effective treatment is available from a veterinarian. Because you cannot automatically assume any discharge is from ear mites, you shouldn't treat with an ear mite medication sold at pet stores; only medicate if your veterinarian recommends it. Accurate diagnosis of the condition will speed your gerbil's recovery and save him from discomfort and pain.

Improper Husbandry

When properly cared for, gerbils are less stressed and have better natural resistance to diseases. A plethora of problems can affect gerbils due to poor husbandry.

A gerbil's front incisor teeth wear down naturally through regular gnawing and chewing.

Gerbil Health Care

Husbandry is a big word for how a pet is taken care of and includes aspects such as housing, food, and water. A gerbil is completely dependent upon you to provide him with the proper environment. Gerbils cannot modify the size, temperature, air circulation, or cleanliness of their home.

Providing a clean cage is one of the most important ways you can help your gerbils stay healthy. Spoiled food and a dirty cage are invitations for illness. Routine cleaning is the most effective method for preventing disease organisms from becoming established in your gerbils' home and overpowering their natural resistance to disease. Your gerbils are most likely to get sick when you become forgetful about cleaning their cage.

Heredity

Between 20 to 40 percent of gerbils develop seizures when they are about two months of age. This condition is inherited and is seen in certain selectively bred lines of gerbils. The seizures are usually over in a few minutes and have no long-term effects.

During a seizure, the gerbil suddenly appears rigid, and usually lies motionless or trembling on the cage floor. Some gerbils outgrow this condition. There is no treatment for seizures, although minimizing stress can reduce the frequency of the seizures.

Aging

As a gerbil gets older, you might begin to notice changes in his behavior and body condition due to aging. Symptoms often appear so gradually in aging animals that pet owners sometimes do not notice. However, middle-aged and older gerbils are more prone to illnesses than when they were young. Non-infectious ailments such as tumors are usually seen in older animals. Old gerbils also have a tendency to gain weight and to groom themselves less frequently; thus, their fur no longer looks as sleek and shiny.